SAP PS FAQ: SAP Project Systems Questions, Answers, and Explanations

SAPCOOKBOOK.COM

Please visit our website at www.sapcookbook.com
© 2006 Equity Press all rights reserved.

ISBN 1-933804-15-7

All rights reserved. No part of this publication may be reproduced, stored in a retrieval system, or transmitted in any form or by any means, electronic, mechanical, photocopying, recording or otherwise, without either the prior written permission of the publisher or a license permitting restricted copying in the United States or abroad.

The programs in this book have been included for instructional value only. They have been tested with care but are not guaranteed for any particular purpose. The publisher does not offer any warranties or representations not does it accept any liabilities with respect to the programs.

Trademark notices

SAP, SAP EBP, SAP SRM, Netweaver, and SAP New Dimension are registered trademarks of SAP AG. This publisher gratefully acknowledges SAP permission to use its trademark in this publication. SAP AG is not the publisher of this book and is not responsible for it under any aspect of the law.

TABLE OF CONTENTS

SAP PS FAQ: SAP Project Systems Questions, Answers, and Explanations vii

Question 1:	Phase Plan hours by month on Internal NWA 1	
Question 2:	PS Authorization 2	
Question 3:	Going back to a Project version 4	
Question 4:	To display budget value in report painter 5	
Question 5:	Classification for WBS elements 7	
Question 6:	Transaction to Reverse a PS Document 8	
Question 7:	Material components for externally processed activities 10	
Question 8:	CATS data report - (standard reports or tables) 11	
Question 9:	Project stock managing 12	
Question 10:	Subcontracting PR from PS 13	
Question 11:	Reapply Standard project definition to created projects 14	
Question 12:	PS Standard reports in ALV format only in version 4.7 15	
Question 13:	Updating z fields on PRPS using BAPI_PROJECT_MAINTAIN 16	
Question 14:	Attach an incoming email to a project 17	
Question 15:	Settlement to assets from level3 18	
Question 16:	When WBS element get updated to cost/revenue posting 20	
Question 17:	CN41 / Layout / Default setting 22	
Question 18:	PS Substitution using user exits 23	
Question 19:	Activity ID 24	
Question 20:	SD x PS 25	
Question 21:	WBS Long Text Report 26	
Question 22:	WorkForce Planning 27	
Question 23:	cProjects or PS? 28	

Question 24:	Tables for plan cost/revenues with actual cost/rev for project	29
Question 25:	Unit costing	30
Question 26:	BOM explosion during BOM transfer	31
Question 27:	BOM Transfer	32
Question 28:	Tentative actual start/finish date	33
Question 29:	depreciation simulation	34
Question 30:	Adding 2 more characters in the Project Coding Mask	35
Question 31:	PS - CATS timesheets for projects	37
Question 32:	Loading Project Structures using LSMW	38
Question 33:	Purchase Requisition in Activities and Material Component	40
Question 34:	Rem Order Plan	42
Question 35:	Processing PR from Project System	44
Question 36:	Dates not overlapping	45
Question 37:	Report CN41 5.0	46
Question 38:	WBS Plan Values Table	47
Question 39:	Settle projects via existing internal orders to final assets	48
Question 40:	User Status	49
Question 41:	Include Validations in Transport Request	50
Question 42:	PS report S_ALR_87013542 - currency	51
Question 43:	Summarization at CN41 data	52
Question 44:	WBS Element xxxx FREI_VERSION already exists	53
Question 45:	Error in CJ9C	55
Question 46:	Confirmation of Actual Cost	56
Question 47:	Configuration of sub networks	57
Question 48:	Required/mandatory fields for Material Component in Project	58
Question 49:	Include Validations in Transport Request	60
Question 50:	A Reservation for every Purchase Requisition in PS	61
Question 51:	"CATA" Time Transfer to Target Components	62

Question 52:	PS confirmation: Activity and Network 63
Question 53:	PS Confirmations 64
Question 54:	Is Network number unique? 65
Question 55:	Value based commitment 66
Question 56:	Project set up under closed cost / profit centers 68
Question 57:	Protect to delete material component item 70
Question 58:	Using CM01, Capacity Evaluation 71
Question 59:	CJ88 and posting date 72
Question 60:	Mass change of user status in projects 73
Question 61:	Assignment if we still need to settle 74
Question 62:	Account assignment in PR for WBS 77
Question 63:	Distribution Cycle 78
Question 64:	CJ91 - Page Down does not work (BDC or not) 79
Question 65:	Remaining Order Plan 80
Question 66:	Basic dates on Project Definition and WBS 83
Question 67:	Creating a network activity using a BAPI 84
Question 68:	Commitment item per WBS 85
Question 69:	Not able to close a project 86
Question 70:	How to create a WBS element 87
Question 71:	A Project with a standard project and network 88
Question 72:	Monthly Budget 89
Question 73:	Settlement Process 91
Question 74:	Conversion of production order from Unrestricted Stock to Project Stock 94
Question 75:	Material Actual Figures 96
Question 76:	AFVC- JEST, JCDS 98
Question 77:	CN23 Relevant Table 99
Question 78:	Restrictions on Availability Control 101
Question 79:	IM/PS transaction IME0 103
Question 80:	Planned revenue 104

Question 81:	Down load PS report in XLS	105
Question 82:	LOE activity	106
Question 83:	BCWS and BCWP not calculated	107
Question 84:	Remove mandatory field, bus area project profile for STD project	108
Question 85:	Milestone completion Report	109
Question 86:	Link between PS and MM	110
Question 87:	Economics for PS	111
Question 88:	Customizing detail screen for Definition project	112
Question 89:	PS report to see all goods movements linked to one project	113
Question 90:	PR and Reservations	114
Question 91:	Project with AUC and Revenue	116
Question 92:	TAC CNB1 or ME5J with ALV	119
Question 93:	Project Coding Mask	120
Question 94:	Capitalization AUC invest measure to asset from project sy	121
Question 95:	Procedure to capitalize AUC inv measure to final asset	122
Question 96:	Project Settlement to Assets	123
Question 97:	Posting actual costs to WBS element and settling to AUC investment measure	124
Question 98:	Configure PReq Doc Type for PS-generated Purchase Requirement	125
Question 99:	Over all Budget and Yearly Budget	126
Index		127

SAP PS FAQ: SAP Project Systems Questions, Answers, and Explanations

SAPCOOKBOOK
Equity Press

SAP Project Systems FAQ

☞ QUESTION 1

Phase Plan hours by month on Internal NWA

Is there a way to plan hours on an internal Activity Element by month or period?

For example: 3000 hours are demanded against the work center:

400 hrs are planned for Jan
500 hrs are planned for Feb
2000 hrs are planned for Mar
100 hrs are planned for Apr

The customer does not wish to have multiple Activities or Activity Elements but requires the ability to phase hours.

✍ ANSWER

Having an activity for each month is very easy and the most logical way to solve this is:

If you need it for cost calculation, try CJR2

SAP Project Systems FAQ

☞ QUESTION 2

PS Authorization

My client has a requirement that two persons are assigned the same roles (e.g. Project manager) in the same Plant and authorized for all project types.

These two persons should be able to view COST/REVENUE reports ONLY for the projects these persons are working on and not for all the projects in the plant.

How do I achieve this?

✍ ANSWER

You need put a new customer object for PS (in this case Plant) transaction PFCG, then give one role for these two persons assigned.

The Enhancement for you to do this is CNEX0002 - PS Authorization check.

If this does not work, try using the same report Enhancement:

S38MREP1 - Exit at Start report
RTR00010 - Exit in report tree (display transactions)

It is necessary to use the same code like:

"AUTHORITY-CHECK OBJECT 'A_S_GSBER'
ID 'BUKRS' FIELD i_bukrs
ID 'GSBER' FIELD wt_tab-gsber."

Assign them in the person responsible field for the project in their project. Then run a report using the dynamic selection on person responsible. I think this will help.

SAP Project Systems FAQ

☞ QUESTION 3

Going back to a Project version

Can I go back to a previous version of a project? For instance, a new project version is created automatically on release of the project. Is it possible to go back to the previous version in order to "undo" the release?

✍ ANSWER

Project versions are used as snapshots of projects at different status or manually triggered points. You would not be able to go back to previous versions because the version is not the operative project.

You will not be able to undo a REL status.

☞ QUESTION 4

To display budget value in report painter

I'm in 46C. I created a report painter using library '6P3'. This report contains column: budget, actual, commitment value, settled amount for project. Which characteristic should I use to display budget?

I initially used characteristic 'value type=21-23' to display commitment value. So I assume that I should use characteristic 'value type=41' to display budget. But budget value did not come out. Can report painter for PS display budget value?

And can Drilldown Report display settlement amount of project?

Furthermore, is there a similar flow for internal order?

✍ ANSWER

You can't see the budget in library 6P3 because it's not integrated in a predefined column, you can see the predefined columns with the transaction GR23, and you can see that the library 6P1 has all that you need about budget.

For drilldown to other reports you need to see the report interface in the group of reports (You need to insert your report in a group), in the header of the group report you can assign other reports like senders or receivers.

The library is used in the project summarization, to see the data you need to make the next steps:

SAP Project Systems FAQ

KKR0 - Create a hierarchy and define a structure inner hierarchy
CJEQ - Import reports for summarization from client '000'
CJH1 - Run Inheritance for all projects
KKRC - Run summarization

But you need to verify if your project profile has checked the check box "Project Summarization".

Yes, there is a similar flow. You can use the transactions: KKR0, CJH1, and KKRC.

You need to look for a transaction similar to CJEQ.

The libraries 6P1 and 6P3 are exclusive for projects; it uses the RPSCO special database for PS.

Check the libraries 6O1, 6O2, and 7O1, may be there are more.

☞ QUESTION 5

Classification for WBS elements

Can I use classification on a WBS element? I don't mean classification for summarization reporting. I want to classify WBS elements the same way you would classify materials.

✍ ANSWER

There is no other way. The "classification for summarization reporting" is the same technique that is applied for materials.

Alternatively you may consider enhancement CNEX0007 to store specific a free data field.

SAP Project Systems FAQ

☞ QUESTION 6

Transaction to Reverse a PS Document

A simple question regarding Budgets:

I have the document number of the entry I need to reverse, but cannot find the TCode to do so. It must be a reversal. I need to reset the BUDG System Status indicator (OPSX) but first need to eliminate the budget values by using the same transaction that was used to put the budget in (CJ30). Unfortunately, the user got the Budget to zero using CJ38. If I can reverse this, then I will be back to where I can achieve my goal.

We are running version 4.6c.

What I need to do is actually reverse the document that was created by the user when they did the return in CJ38. I need to carry out a reversal to get the BUDG indicator to come off (reset) on the WBS (OPSX) so I can adjust the WBS Structure.

What transaction is used (or, is it possible) to reverse a Budget Return in Project (CJ38)?

✍ ANSWER

The return is done using a negative entry in CJ38.

For example: If you had a return of $100.00 and want to make a return, just enter $100.00- to reverse it and vice-versa.

It seems to me that you are trying to delete the document physically and that can be done in two ways:

1) Delete transactional data. It will only work if your cocd is not set as productive. However, I don't recommend this approach in production.

2) Archiving -that might be the only way for you to get rid of the documents. Reversals will always generate documents and you will lock yourself on it.

☞ QUESTION 7

Material components for externally processed activities

What is the use and purpose of material components for externally processed network activities?

✍ ANSWER

Generally, material components are either internally acquired from production or inventory, or externally acquired from vendors. But the answer to your question depends on whether or not you are using valuated project stock, or no project stock in your PS settings. If you are using no stock, you would likely be acquiring all materials from vendors and expending them directly to the project. I ordinarily use an internal procurement activity for this purpose and add my material components to the internal activity. (This allows me to also assign internal labor cost to the activity of procurement.) If the Reservation/Purchase Requirement setting on the activity or component is "Immediately", a requisition will be generated for the materials when you save the project. The Procurement Type setting on the component should be either Requisition + reservation for WBS element, in which case you'll get both a reservation and a requisition number, or 3rd Party requisition, in which case you'll get only a requisition number.

You can also use an external activity for this, but you must then assign a cost to the external activity of procurement, rather than picking up an internal labor activity rate.

You assign components the same way.

SAP Project Systems FAQ

☞ QUESTION 8

CATS data report - (standard reports or tables)

We are using CATS to capture labor costs in projects, the time entry is for the WBS elements. Once the time is approved, I can see the labor costs in CJI3 report but when I check for the data in tables AFRU, CATSDB, CATSPS I do not see the postings. I can get the data from tables CATSCO and COVP.

Is there something that I am missing in the process?

Why is the data not getting populated in the tables CATSDB and CATSPS?

I checked with the standard report S_ALR_87015071 and the time entry is not available. Does time entry get populated in this report?

✍ ANSWER

Confirmation on WBS cannot result in a time confirmation, which is stored in AFRU (for networks, PM orders).

The time postings against WBS elements would be a CO posting.

SAP Project Systems FAQ

☞ QUESTION 9

Project stock managing

There is a company with two plants named A and B. Plant B produce some parts for A. Plant A does the assembly with parts from B and others purchased.

The project is managed with valuated stock. The parts requirement by plant A (which is produced by B) will trigger a transfer order; Plant B will run MPR and then create a production order for the transfer order. The problem is: the raw material for those production orders are still managed by "valuated stock".

The company needs Plant B to NOT manage production order in valuation project stock, because the raw materials are something like steel pipe, and steel board. All the projects can use it. It is crazy to control those in project stock.

How do I resolve this issue?

✍ ANSWER

For those materials which you wish to manage on plant stock level only, set up value 2 in the MRP4-Individual/coll - field.

☞ QUESTION 10

Subcontracting PR from PS

I want to generate subcontracting PR from the project system. Presently, the system is not showing any subcontracting check in external or services activities.

Is it possible to generate subcontracting PR from PS.? If so, how can it be done?

What are the settings for that?

✍ ANSWER

It looks like you want to generate a requirement for subcontract work from PS. This must be done using an external network activity. You'll have to describe the service and provide the price, procurement group information, etc, as required. The systems will guide you through this. Assign the activity to the pertinent WBS element and the commitment will be assigned there.

There is one other critical setting you must make. On the external activity External tab, the Reservation/Purchasing Requirement field must be set to "immediately" if you want a requirement generated. If it is set to "From Release", the requirement will be generated when the activity is released. If it is set to "Never", no requirement will be generated.

Or if you need detailed follow up on the progress of subcontractors work, you may consider using External Services requisition at the project.

SAP Project Systems FAQ

☞ QUESTION 11

Reapply Standard project definition to created projects

We have a project definition containing all structures of a product. One structure was summarized to one WBS in STD structure because it was subcontracted to a supplier.

We will now produce this part in-house and need to explode this WBS with its own structure.

Is there a way to automatically "update" all current projects with the new structure or automatically "create" all missing WBS?

✍ ANSWER

In standard CJ20N based functionality, this is not possible.

If the volume is really high, you can consider Variant configuration for standard networks or alternatively LSMW or ECATT entry tool usage.

To consider these, you would need a volume in thousands, because the copy of the desired WBS (with substructure) doesn't take many seconds manually, once you have done it for the first project.

Try using CNMASS to do mass changes to Projects.

☞ QUESTION 12

PS Standard reports in ALV format only in version 4.7

In version 4.7, SAP GUI 620, svc level 57, all of my PS reports show in ALV format only. Does anyone know how to get these reports to show in the standard format?

I am not able to drill down in any PS reports to either line items or source documents. Is this GUI related?

✍ ANSWER

The graphical view can be set in transaction CJE2 -> Change Report Settings. Select the report number, for example 12KST1C. Then select the "Output Type" tab. Elect "Available on Selection Screen". Then save it and transport it if necessary. You will get the option to elect the classic graphic view in the report selection screen.

SAP Project Systems FAQ

☞ QUESTION 13

Updating z fields on PRPS using BAPI_PROJECT_MAINTAIN

I'm creating WBS Elements using BAPI_PROJECT_MAINTAIN and its working fine. However, I need to update bespoke Z fields that were created in PRPS also and there is no extension on this BAPI to facilitate this.

What is the best way to do this? Will I have to update PRPS directly?

✍ ANSWER

As you have noted, there is no extension to do this. However, you can use the "USER FIELDS" together with a substitution to copy from user fields to Z fields when you save the project (CJ20N Edit/Substitution).

☞ QUESTION 14

Attach an incoming email to a project

Is it possible to attach an incoming email to a project on PS from the business workplace of SAP?

✍ ANSWER

If you just want to attach the incoming email, save the email in a local folder in message format and attach it as a document (if DMS is activated).

You can also copy the email and paste to a PS text in a WBS.

☞ QUESTION 15

Settlement to assets from level3

We are collecting costs at WBS level3 elements and want to settle costs to the Asset.

I need to clarify the following to proceed with the requirement:

1. Do I need to attach the investment profile (which we are doing manually) for all the WBS elements (to AUC) including level1 and level2s or is it enough to attach the investment profile only to level3 WBS elements?

2. I understand that an AUC will be created for each of level3 WBS elements and when I run the settlement for level1 WBS element in CJ88 (using with hierarchy option), the settlement will work fine irrespective of whether I have attached investment profiles to level1 or level2.

    Can I put project definition instead of level 1 WBS element?

3. I have settled the WBS element costs to an AUC but do I need to use CJIC to settle the costs finally to an asset for the same WBS element?

✍ ANSWER

Answers are given in the order they were asked:

1. You can attach investment profile manually to the 3rd level (may be last level) WBS element only, if you are collecting actual cost at that level, no need to assign investment profile at level 1 & 2.

SAP Project Systems FAQ

2. If you are having predefined investment profile for a project profile, you can maintain it in project profile in TCode OPSA. System will create AUC for the WBS element which is account assigned only. You need to keep only 3rd level WBS elements account assigned.

    Yes, you can use WBS definition in settlement. You do need to specify asset value date.

3. Automatic capitalization of your asset will be done on project TECO. You can also partially capitalize with CJ88 option 3. Don't forget the asset value date. You do have to maintain settlement rule to final asset.

QUESTION 16

When WBS element get updated to cost/revenue posting

We are using valuated sales order stock with back to back PO from SD. We are now setting up WBS to track project revenue and cost which consist of several sales orders bundled together.

In the sales order line item I have inputted the WBS element but while triggering PR and converting to PO, the system says the stock account cannot be directly posted with the WBS element. Then I realized that the stock account is not a P/L account and therefore should not be posted against a WBS element. Now my question is, when can a WBS element get posted to? Is it during posting goods issue?

As of this time, we do not want to use project stock yet.

What about the expense material that we directly expended out for the project? Will the WBS element get posted to during the process of goods receipt?

Should the WBS element be entered into the header or line item in SO?

What is the implication?

ANSWER

First, when using the WBS element in creating a SO, the price of the SO is posted as 'planning' in the WBS element.

The actual SO will be posted as revenue when billing.

The goods cost and expenses will be posted as commitment (if using commitment); When creating the PO (if purchased items), the actual will be posted when doing goods receipt. Depending on your setting you can configure it to be received directly to the SO, so it gets even better for analysis.

Secondly, when entering a WBS element in a SO, if you enter at header level all line items will be charged to that specific project.

When entering at line item, it gives you a flexibility to have a different WBS element for each line item or as no WBS element in certain line items.

The last case example is:

In a SO to sell a make-to-order product using PS, the first line item has the WBS element. The second is parts (made to stock items) to be sold together and they do not need a project.

QUESTION 17

CN41 / Layout / Default setting

On CN41 I have built a default layout for users (Flag "default setting" when saving layout). However, I don't want this flag removed by users if they try to save it, and more than that, I don't want them to be able to save this layout. I only want to enable them to create their own layout without modifying the one viewed by default.

How can I be able to configure this?

ANSWER

Use transaction OPTU -> create separate profile for displayed fields and assign to the overall profile.

I am referring to SAP version ECC 5.0.

☞ QUESTION 18

PS Substitution using user exits

I need to default a cost center into the responsible cost center field on a project. This need for default is to be based on which responsible person is entered on the project.

I am thinking of using a substitution with a user exit, but I am not familiar with it.

How do we write the user exit to be used in the substitution?

✍ ANSWER

Your requirement is standard substitution capability. Just define prerequisites PRPS-VERNR (person responsible) and substitution field PRPS-FKOKR.

Another solution you can use is the WBS field selection by using influences function.

Add a normal validation in front of this or make the person responsible field required to ensure you got a field to look from.

☞ QUESTION 19

Activity ID

How much range can an activity ID have and where is it maintained?

In my case:

cn>> internal processing>> activity id >>0010

✍ ANSWER

Use TCode- OPUU; Under N/w parameters find Op.act. incrmt.

☞ QUESTION 20

SD x PS

My client opened a new project to integrate PS with SD.

Here are some questions:

1) How do I create an automatic sales Quotation based in a PS project?

2) How do I create an automatic Sales order based in a PS Project?

✍ ANSWER

There are ways to generate a network in PS from SD sales order. There is some standard SAP transaction available for that.

However, there is no setting in PS by which you can generate Quotation or Order automatically using the same (PS). But you can create sales quotation or order with reference to the project or you may use DIP profile to do the same function.

An alternative solution will be to use functionality resources related billing. Use ODP1 profile to customize the link between SD/CO and PS.

For more options, go to:

http://help.sap.com/saphelp_46c/helpdata/fr/aa/96853478616434e10000009b38f83b/frameset.htm

☞ QUESTION 21

WBS Long Text Report

Is there a report which shows the Long Texts for each WBS element?

✎ ANSWER

Use function module READ_TEXT for retrieving long text.

☞ QUESTION 22

WorkForce Planning

We are using CMP2 for doing workforce planning in our Organization. We attached resources to activities. We want to put an end date to the resource attached so that the particular resource does not appear in cmp2.

We have tried attaching resource to WBS too but it doesn't work.

Is there any configuration needed to achieve our purpose? If so, how do we do it?

✎ ANSWER

In CMP2, mark the relevant line then press the bottom with the pencil. Make a new end date and save.

Next time you enter CMP2 the start date has to be after the end date you entered.

Be aware that the end date affects the work list for the person in CATS.

☞ QUESTION 23

cProjects or PS?

What would be the advantage of choosing standard PS functionality instead of cProjects functionality?

✍ ANSWER

Both can do the same function, but "cProjects" can do more.

"cProjects" provides Stage Gate Methodology project management of documented deliverables. It is mainly suitable for a New Product Introduction.

Project System provides project planning and project accounting mainly for Engineering projects managed according to a large program of activities within a standardized Work Breakdown Structure.

☞ QUESTION 24

Tables for plan cost/revenues with actual cost/rev for project

I need to write an ABAP code for plan profit versus actual profit for projects in a company code/plant. For this I need to find the plan/actual revenues and plan/ actual cost for projects.

Which tables will give me the plan and actual revenues as well as cost per period?

✍ ANSWER

Various tables are maintained for the planned cost based on the planning type. You can try RPSCO for your requirement.

I assume that you are in TCS.

If network costing is also done then you need to go to the following tables as well: COSS for secondary costs and COSP for primary costs;

☞ QUESTION 25

Unit costing

We are using 4.7. For the initial plan, we are using unit costing for WBS elements in the Project where we are mainly specifying materials.

Is there any report which will show me the consolidated material requirement generated from unit costing for a particular project?

If no standard report is available, which tables do I need to refer for development?

✍ ANSWER

I don't think there is any such report. However, for development purposes, you can use table CKIS.

Use transaction CNS52 where you can find material-wise quantity (Requirements Quantity) and unit price (Price in Local Currency). Just download to Excel and put the formula Qty *. 'Price' will give the cost of all materials.

☞ QUESTION 26

BOM explosion during BOM transfer

I have a problem of BOM explosion while assigning the material with Multi-level BOM thru transaction CN33. After the BOM transfer thru CN33, only the header level material with single level items get assigned to project activity and not the material component from second level and so on.

Examples:

> A is Header material;
> X is 1st level child item;
> X1 2nd level;
> X2 2nd level;
> Y is the multilevel BOM;

Only material A with X & Y gets transferred to Projects & not the X1 & X2.

What could be the possible reason for this issue?

✍ ANSWER

In the selection criteria (Shift+F5) you have to choose the Multi-level if the Reference Point is maintained for all the materials attached to the BOM at all levels. Select all items if the reference point is not maintained for all the materials at the lower level.

SAP Project Systems FAQ

☞ QUESTION 27

BOM Transfer

I want to affect components on my network with the BOM explosion in order to have a link between my network and my BOM.

How have I to access the reference point?

Is the "reference point" a key between BOM and PS activity, and does it have another impact?

What is the function of these configurations below?

Follow IMG points: ("Define Profiles for Bill Of Material Transfer", "Define Reference Points for BOM Transfer", "Define Fields in BOM and Activity as Reference Point");

✍ ANSWER

Yes. The reference points works as the matching point. You have to define the Reference point (say ABCD) in IMG. Then while creating the BOM you have to give the reference point (ABCD) for the Materials in BOM and ref. point (ABCD) for the Activity where you want the BOM to be transferred.

☞ QUESTION 28

Tentative actual start/finish date

The tentative actual start/finish date is copied from the confirmation of activities for the WBS element. However, the WBS in the upper level of other WBS with activities doesn't get these dates updated. Is this possible to calculate these dates like the system does in Basic and Forecast Dates? Or is it only the WBS elements that have activities directly assigned can have these dates updated?

✐ ANSWER

In project planning board, carry out "determine actual date" followed by "extrapolate dates" function.

☞ QUESTION 29

Depreciation simulation

When I make depreciation simulation in IM (transaction S_ALR_87010178) the system makes a simulation both on investment costs and overhead costs. Overhead costs are given in the variant of the master record of the appropriation request.

We only activate the investment costs so I only want those costs visible in the simulation report.

How I can I split these two values?

✍ ANSWER

The solution is in note 865080.

QUESTION 30

Adding 2 more characters in the Project Coding Mask

If I add two more characters at the end of the Project Coding Mask, will there be an effect on the projects already created using that mask?

For example, I already created a project with the name PROJ-1 and its coding mask is PROJ-X. I want to name the new project that I'll create as PROJ-111. The new mask will now be PROJ-XXX.

I just found out that the length of a coding mask cannot be changed anymore if it had already been used in past projects.

I also tried deleting a coding mask and re-entering a new length of the same prefix but unfortunately, it still recognizes the original length that it had earlier.

How do I resolve this?

ANSWER

You should be doing configuration in one client and transporting in a production (working) client.

You can change it in the above scenario. You may face some problems to open old projects, if position of separator changed. For this problem, there is OSS note to rectify (change) old project codes

You have to change the project code of all the projects where this coding mask is used. Afterwards, you can then change the coding mask in Configuration. The system allows for this.

But if the number of existing projects is high, it is unusual to change the project codes in the production environment. Rather, create one more coding mask which can be used in future.

QUESTION 31

PS - CATS timesheets for projects

We use CATS timesheet to capture times for projects. Is there a way to block users from entering times in 2005 on the time sheet?

We only want them to enter times in 2006, and not be able to enter hours for a 2005 date.

ANSWER

One of the CATS customer exits can be used for that. Look in SMOD for CATS.

The most likely way to do this would be by locking the prior period to postings which will happen in the normal course of business anyway. This function is generally controlled by the FICO folks who control period end financial closing activities. It is routine that they would lock the prior period and open the current period to postings. At year end the same thing would happen. So I don't think you'll have a problem with this in production. In development, these things are not as disciplined. But you can coordinate this with FICO in development to make it happen. The transaction needed is to open and close posting periods S_ALR_87003642. This is not an IMG transaction. The path to it is Accounting-> FI-> GL-> Environment-> Current settings-> Open and Close posting periods.

SAP Project Systems FAQ

☞ QUESTION 32

Loading Project Structures using LSMW

I am trying to use LSMW to load a number of WBS elements within one project structure. The system assigns a unique version of the 'Level' field PRPS-STUFE for every WBS element entered. For example: Line 1 = PRPS-STUFE (01) Line 2 = PRSP-STUFE (02) etc. When I have more than one element at level 2, level 3 etc., the system is not smart enough to assign a WBS to a level based on the data in the spreadsheet. The only way around it is to have a one to one relationship between the unique STUFE field and the WBS element I want to load. This would make for an extremely large spreadsheet though.

Before I proceed with this tedious task and write an ABAP to perform it, is there any other known solution to this problem?

✍ ANSWER

This is a "known problem" with PS conversions, but a couple of options exist.

The most efficient is that the projects are created by copying from template (LSMW run 1 for CJ20), and as second step maintained for individual WBS (LSMW run 2 for CJ20), where e.g. WBS data can be maintained and underlying activities added, but even for the second one, you face a problem if the activity lists/structures vary a lot in quantity and levels.

The bottom line is that if the projects to be imported do not fit into templates, the system should have the same logic structurally. Programming the LSMW or ECATT requires so much, that it doesn't make sense for below 1000 projects. In this specific case for 100-150 projects, if a "copy from template" approach doesn't work, the most efficient solution by far is a column wise 'copy-paste', grouped in advance like it is done in Excel.

There are some other options you could take:

You can use LSMW in a different way to upload the project in 4.7:

1. Create project definition & Level 1 WBS & one Level 2 WBS element manually;

2. Now while carrying out recording for LSMW in cj02, use Insert Line option above Level 2;

3. In the Excel file, Keep all the down below WBS elements at level 2 only;

4. After uploading the complete file, carry out function "Derive Structure" for project;

This method is useful if you are copying the coding mask of a superior WBS into subordinate WBS elements.

QUESTION 33

Purchase Requisition in Activities and Material Component

I need to understand the PR in networks. I have created external activities and assigned material components. I have set the PR to Release immediately in the activities. To release the activities I need to fill in the purchasing information (material group, purchasing group, etc.) When I release the activities it creates 2 requisitions, one for the activities and one for material components. Is this the right way to set it up or should I set the Activities PR to "Never". When I set it up to "Never" it creates only a PR for the material component.

Can we use internal activities for external procurement (Purchasing materials from outside vendors)?

When do we use external activities?

ANSWER

External activity = task you purchase, and thus you get a PR, e.g. subcontracting work. If this is not your intention, use the internal activity instead, and assign your materials there. Afterwards, you will get PR's only for those.

Internal activity is used just to collect the components which are to be purchased. The activity need not have any other function, but may have them when needed.

The 'External activity' you may use as part of the overall scheduling/planning, when you purchase the whole activity, e.g. Design work, Installation work, Transportation etc. from an external subcontractor.

☞ QUESTION 34

Rem Order Plan

In cost report "Plan/actual/commitment/rem. plan/assigned" (PS infosystem), I find values filled for rem.plan at WBS elements level. We do not have any postings to WBS elements except budgets.

Even though Rem. Plan is 0 at order level, it does show some dollar amounts at WBS elements. Again Orders are our cost objects.

I was wondering if that standard report is invalid in our case.

In my report I do see the ROP as $0 at the order level, whereas at WBS Element level (which is supposed to add up the amounts on the IOs under it) I do see some value. We do not have any posting on WBS; they get actual costs summed up from the IOs.

I have observed this scenario only when the dollar amount for the actual is negative.

For Example:

    Object------Actual----Comm----ROP:

        WBS1 -100 0 100;
        Order A 200 0 0;
        Order B 300 0 0;

Its value type is 25 and it is in structure CCSS.

Could there be any setting that would/could lead to incorrect ROP values?

✐ ANSWER

No, the report is valid. The remaining order plans are comprised of planned labour, stock reservations or unrelease material components, all at the order level. It is reduced through timekeeping entries, stock issues and material requisitions. Remaining order plan can also show up if a PO line item has been deleted without the material component in the order being deleted. The remaining order plan can also show up if an item has been ordered and received and then transferred out via a journal entry.

ROP is always only visible on the WBS level.

For what it's worth, the concept of ROP is very confusing to both consultants and clients. SAP has offered a fix to eliminate it from all standard PS reports. Look for it in the OSS notes.

SAP Project Systems FAQ

☞ QUESTION 35

Processing PR from Project System

When I am trying to process any PR (either services or Material) the system is giving this error message:

G/L account 410000 cannot be used (please correct)
Message no. ME045

Diagnosis:

Comparison of the field selection strings from the G/L account 410000 and the account assignment category P reveals that there is an incompatible combination of field selections for the field selection group 'Earmarked Funds'.

The G/L account field selection is stored in table T004F; that for the account assignment is stored in table T162K.

It is giving a same error with all the g/l.

I checked the field status group of g/l and account assignment P. I did not find any inconsistency in Field selection.

What could be the problem and how do I resolve it?

✍ ANSWER

First, check if the field status group is set properly for using this account in PS.

Second, make the earmarked funds filed active in filed status group.

SAP Project Systems FAQ

☞ QUESTION 36

Dates not overlapping

I keep receiving this message: "NO overlapping dates found".

This message is not allowing me to save the project.

How can this be resolved?

✍ ANSWER

You must be doing top-down scheduling. There must be inconsistencies in the dates of WBS and network activities. For that project to go through, correct them manually. Also check the Planning board settings in Project profile configurations.

You might also want to check some OSS notes available for this message.

SAP Project Systems FAQ

☞ **QUESTION 37**

Report CN41 5.0

How can I change the report CN41 and then save it in the new version 5.0?

I changed the layout, added columns, and changed fields. However, I don't know how I can save the new variant. I would like to see it when I open the CN41.

What is the difference between CN41 and CNS41? How can I get rid of the Grids in CNS41?

How do I save display variants?

✎ **ANSWER**

You can save layout as per your requirement and recall it whenever required. I hope your requirement is to see certain fields/columns only.

You can use OPTU to customize the required fields and then at CN41 "Get Profile/Variant" and choose the desired Sub profile for Displayed fields.

It is not possible to dynamically save a displayed field list variant and in ALV reports.

SAP Project Systems FAQ

☞ QUESTION 38

WBS Plan Values Table

If I plan by WBS using CJ40, where can I see the table which stores these values?

✍ ANSWER

If you are using structure planning, you can get in the RPSCO table. If you are using cost element planning, you can get in COSS & COSP tables. You have to select proper value type in these tables.

You can also use other tables such as BPEJ/BPEG/BPGE.

SAP Project Systems FAQ

☞ QUESTION 39

Settle projects via existing internal orders to final assets

Up until now we have been using internal orders to follow up our projects. Now we're installing PS for a better follow up. How can we link the existing internal orders to the new WBS elements and later on settling the WBS elements to final assets for the values which were posted to the internal orders?

✍ ANSWER

You can settle the internal order with the corresponding WBS elements (may be by cost elements for proper tracking of original cost element) or you can try reposting.

☞ QUESTION 40

User Status

We have created a User Status to make the project code field uneditable. Unlike the system status, we are not able to reverse the User status.

How can this be done?

For example: System status TECO can be reversed to REL.

✍ ANSWER

You can manage the reverse user status from lowest and highest status and a combination with the authorization object.

QUESTION 41

Include Validations in Transport Request

I have created the Validations in customizing client. When I clicked save, the system gave message 'ABAP code generated successfully'. But it is not asking for Transport request.

How can I include this configuration into a transport request?

ANSWER

It does not come automatically. The transport of validation is a process. In the validation screen go Validation --> Transport. Click on this and it will ask for the validation to be transported. Give your validation and save it.

QUESTION 42

PS report S_ALR_87013542 - currency

Is it possible to see the results of this report in different currencies?

ANSWER

Try following the menu path Edit/Currency translation.

☞ QUESTION 43

Summarization at CN41 data

I'm working in 4.6 PS and I need the data to show at CN41 (costs, revenues, etc) be with summarization an top or bottom line

Is it possible?

✍ ANSWER

If you choose to see summarized data in the report, the line for the project will be showing the sum of values.

Another solution is to export the data to Excel and make the sum there.

☞ QUESTION 44

WBS Element xxxx FREI_VERSION already exists

We are currently on 4.6c.

A project definition was created and saved with profiles that we have used successfully in the past.

When the project definition was re-opened and an attempt was made to add a level 1 WBS the following error was encountered

"WBS element xxxx version FREI_VERSION already exists" Message no. CJ 026.

If a system search is made for the WBS that is supposed to "already exist", the system reports that it does not exist.

How do I fix this?

✍ ANSWER

It sounds like customizing is set to make a project version automatically (that could be when a certain system status is set).

If this version is created - the WBS-element can still be deleted in the "original" project. It is not possible if you try to make a new WBS-element with the same ID (and with the status that tells that a project version is to be made). You can not find the WBS-element in the same tables as the

SAP Project Systems FAQ

"original/operative project" - because version data is stored in separate tables.

Instead, try to run a report (example CN41) for the project or WBS-element number where you select version data in the DB-profile - and write the version key that you indicated in your question. That should show you that a version exists. Therefore, you cannot create a new WBS-element with the same key.

☞ QUESTION 45

Error in CJ9C

While running the transaction CJ9C I am getting the following message:

Primary cost element 620601 is not supported in secondary cost planning.

Message # is GM072.

How can this be resolved?

✍ ANSWER

You can refer to SAP Note # 604138.

QUESTION 46

Confirmation of Actual Cost

The actual cost through activity element confirmation (activity type + Cost centre) is not showing up at the activity element level.

How can this be made to display actual cost at the activity element level itself?

ANSWER

On exploration at the service portal of SAP, the following note is needed to be updated to correctly post the actual at element with note 643773.

☞ QUESTION 47

Configuration of sub networks

We are on 4.6c and we need to have the ability to create sub networks in Project Systems.

What would I have to do in SPRO in order for us to activate this functionality?

✍ ANSWER

All the configurations are the same as that of the main network except that you should make configurations in TCode OPTP. This is where you have to assign the sub network type to the main network and control key.

QUESTION 48

Required/mandatory fields for Material Component in Project

We want to set the following fields below as "Required/ mandatory" on the Material Component detail screen in Project System (on the General Data Tab).

Recipient - [RESBD -WEMPF]
Unloading Point - [RESBD-ABLAD]
Storage Location - [RESBD-LGORT]

I have not been able to find a customizing option to set this on the material component level.

Note: The Material Component is attached to the Network Activity.

Is there a customizing option available as per requirements?

ANSWER

Configurations are as follows:

1. If you have separate document type for PR's of PS, it is assigned with field selection group in MM configuration. In IMG Menu you can find it under Materials Management --> Purchasing --> Purchase Requisition --> Define Document Types.

2. The field selection group is defined in the following node under MM purchasing -- Purchase requisition.

SAP Project Systems FAQ

3. Define Screen Layout at Document Level

4. You can make mandatory display etc. in the screen layout which will be assigned to PR document type.

SAP Project Systems FAQ

☞ QUESTION 49

Include Validations in Transport Request

I have created the Validations in customizing client. When I clicked save, system gave message ABAP code generated successfully. But it is not asking for Transport request.

How can I include this configuration together with a transport request?

✍ ANSWER

Choose validation (not step), click validation > Transport. From there you can generate the function requirement successfully.

- 60 -

☞ QUESTION 50

A Reservation for every Purchase Requisition in PS

I have noted that every time we create a Purchase Requisition through the Project System, a Reservation is also automatically being created with account assignment the same as that of the Network and with multiple line items (equivalent to the number of material components created in PS).

What is the rational behind this? Is it due to an error in the configuration, or is this normal?

Furthermore, on clicking on any of the line items (MB25) the following message is prompted:

"Document does not contain any items"

To test this scenario:

1. Create a material component is PS (Network header assigned)
2. Save Project
3. T-Code MB25, enter Network number, Execute.

You have a reservation with a single line item created.

How can this be corrected?

✍ ANSWER

This is not to be confused with a stock reservation. This is perfectly normal and has no negative impact that I know of.

☞ QUESTION 51

"CATA" Time Transfer to Target Components

I have posted Actual Hours (time) in Timesheet "CATSXT", and then I have transferred this time to PS and HR through transaction "CATA" and saved it.

I would like to transfer back these Actual Hours from the target components to timesheet. Is there a reverse transaction for "CATA" which I can take back the Actual Hours that are posted and transferred?

Is there a way to cancel the time transferred?

I need to reverse because I have transferred few project normal man hours for (January) to PS after FI settled all (January) project costs and made the balance zero for January period end closing. As a result, they have costs remaining in the balance. They asked me to remove all the extra costs.

✍ ANSWER

I don't believe that there is a way you can simply reverse the time that has been transferred. I think the only way you can deal with this is to amend the time and then re-transfer it back into the target components, which should cancel the previous postings in favor of the new ones.

Do cancel in CATS and transfer cancellation to PS (can also enter posting date for cancellation to be able to post in open posting period).

☞ QUESTION 52

PS confirmation: Activity and Network

I have confirmed (on CJ20N Project builder) only one activity on my network.

Status is totally confirmed "CNF" and not partially confirmed "PCNF".

Why is this happening?

Did I forget to do something?

✎ ANSWER

Parameter 'Confirmation' in control key of network activities is set to space.

Confirmation is possible, but not necessary.

QUESTION 53

PS Confirmations

We use CATS to capture times. The times are transferred to PS via a nightly batch job. We have instances where the activity on the project gets flagged CNF (final confirmation) automatically.

Why does this happen?

Why is it that when activities are set to complete, no remaining work and final confirmations are made?

ANSWER

Have you checked if your CATS-confirmations have "Confirmed" as default instead of "Partially confirmed"?

Take a look at confirmation parameter. Final confirmation can be defaulted during transfer to PS.

☞ QUESTION 54

Is Network number unique?

Is the network number unique?

Can two different projects have a network with the same number?

Or, are network numbers unique across all projects?

✍ ANSWER

Network numbers can be internally assigned or externally assigned by the user or it can be done by order type.

Yes, the network number is unique, but it is identified by internal number.

☞ QUESTION 55

Value based commitment

Can we have commitment value based on value and not on Quantity?

Where can I activate it?

Presently the commitment reduces to zero as soon as the full quantity is delivered against a project. We want to change it.

The commitments are reducing to zero on doing IV. Final Invoice is not checked in POs.

We are using EA for both Services and Materials and in case of services it is working fine. The Value based commitment is not activated for EA at present.

I tried one scenario for a material (Value based commitment is activated for the unit of measure in CUNI).

I created a PO for 25 quantities USD100 each. CJI5 report commitment: 2500.
GR for 1 quantity, CJI5: 2400, CJI3 (actual): 100.Did MIRO for it for 200, CJI5 becomes 2300.

GR for 24 quantities, CJI5:0.00, CJI3: 2500, MIRO: 500, CJI5:0.00. Should CJI5 not show 2500-(200+500) = 1800 instead of 0.00?

✍ Answer

In Service POs, it shows Value only, not materials.

Use the transaction CUNI (unit of measurement) where you can set how the commitment has to be reduced (thru value/qty).

For the rest of your issues, use funds management for the purpose.

SAP Project Systems FAQ

☞ QUESTION 56

Project set up under closed cost / profit centers

Can Projects be set up under closed cost centers and profit centers?

If I assign an inactive / locked one to the Project, the system should pop up an error message as it goes inactive or locked.

But in my case the system allows to assign inactive / locked profit and cost centers to new projects. This not needed in my case.

✍ ANSWER

First of all, a cost center or a profit center cannot be deleted if it has the valid records.

Now, if you assign a deleted one to the Project, the system will stop throwing an error message as it doesn't exist.

The way to get a message based on a rule you define is Validations. Create a Validation to check the Cost Center locks:

Tools -> Accelerated SAP -> Customizing -> Edit Project;
SAP Reference IMG;

Project System -> Structures -> Operative Structures -> Work Breakdown Structure -> Maintain Validations;

Validations -> WBS Element;
Create Validation;
Create Step;

Prerequisite Cost Center <> "";
Check User Exit;
User Exit looks for lock fields in cost center and checks are not set;
Message User defined - go to Environment menu to define;

QUESTION 57

Protect to delete material component item

I have GI of material components in WBS. But these line items can be deleted.

How can I protect this problem?

ANSWER

Check with your AMT as I am sure it can be very well possible through Authorizations.

Change profile in IMG. According to the document, when we set error in change profile and specify in network parameter, the system will prohibit withdrawal of item.

SAP Project Systems FAQ

☞ QUESTION 58

Using CM01, Capacity Evaluation

We use CM01 to final confirm network activities and PM orders when work is completed. However, when actual hours meet or exceed planned hours, the objects drop off the CM01 view.

Is there a work around or solution for this?

Take the order scenario out of it and just look at the list of capacities. Once you have fulfilled the "planned" capacity, the item drops off the list.

How do you prevent an item from dropping off the list just because you've gone past the "planned" capacity?

✐ ANSWER

First, don't abuse a capacity evaluation transaction for an order closing functionality. If you really need to see networks and pm-orders in one overview, create a query based on CAUFV.

Start CM01, chose work center and before entering you can change some parameters by following the menu-path:

Settings > general > Requirements > category: 1 (Planned requirements);

After that you will see the fulfilled items in the list, too.

☞ QUESTION 59

CJ88 and posting date

Does anyone know how to put posting date from menu Extras -> Posting date to foreground screen, for transaction CJ88 (periodic settlement)?

Is it possible to create display variants for this transaction with included posting date on screen?

Are there any other solutions like a user exit?

✍ ANSWER

You must make the modification in standard screen. You can use transaction variants to input default posting date or make it mandatory.

For creating the transaction variant, use the TCode shd0.

QUESTION 60

Mass change of user status in projects

We currently use either the project builder cj20n or Project Planning Board cj2b to change the user status in the projects. However, this procedure is cumbersome when you want to simultaneously change a number of projects.

Is there a more efficient transaction or procedure for user status change at the activity level (Collective or mass change)?

ANSWER

If you want more options to obtain your objective for collective or simultaneous mass change of projects, you have to write a program that uses CNMASS.

Or another option would be to try LSMW.

QUESTION 61

Assignment if we still need to settle

These problems might sound basic but it is interesting.

1. What is the difference between assigned orders and settlement?

   To elaborate on the situation, here is some background information:

   My network is assigned to WBS Element.

   Do I need to settle it to the same WBS Element (so that costs get attached to the WBS Element) if I need to do the settlement of the same?

   If I need to, then what is the purpose of assigning Network to the WBS Element?

   It gets confusing because I see the costs of Network against WBS Element in cost reports without settlement also.

2. Does the same rule apply to any Order attached to WBS Element?

   What is the Assignment required for?

As far as PM PS is concerned, we are doing a settlement of PM orders to AUC. WBS elements are being used for reporting purpose only.

✏ ANSWER

A network activity should be assigned to your WBS and should also settle to it. The WBS can then settle to a G/L account, Fixed Asset record, Cost Centre or to another WBS if configured correctly. This process will in turn manage your cost flows and integration to their modules.

Assigning an order to a WBS facilitates the hierarchical cost reporting and technical reporting of a project. Technically, you do not have to settle back to the WBS for the system to correctly report the project costs. For example, we use projects and plant maintenance orders to facilitate the cost reporting of major plant maintenance projects. We could have configured the maintenance orders to settle to the WBS and then the WBS to a cost centre. But as any number of maintenance order types (that normally settle to cost centers) might be used in this scenario, we chose not to change the process. So the PM orders settle directly to cost centers and the project cost reporting comes from the order assignments.

Corollary to this, we use a different process for capital projects. We ensure all orders (network and maintenance orders) are assigned to and settle to the WBS. The PS Info system is smart enough to know that costs will show in the project structure because of the assignment and also that costs will show from the settlement. Is this double accounting? No it isn't. It is because the system recognizes the two sources and offsets (or 'cancels') one source for reporting purposes.

For most normal situations you might want to assign and settle your orders to the WBS. This will make life easier for your users as interpreting the cost reports and analyzing cost flows will be understandable because of the rule. Not to mention it should strictly enforce your company's capitalization policies.

Meanwhile, I can see using some PM orders for small capital projects where you might not want to employ project management tools and techniques. For all others, I would recommend settling the cost to the WBS. For starters you would have the aggregated costs (of all those orders) settling to AUC by your lowest level WBS element. If you define your WBS according to your deliverable, then your AM reporting is also improved.

What you are doing is really against SAP design and you are not taking full advantage of the integration and full functionality of PS.

We are also using the Investment Management module to manage our capital program and expense programs where projects are being used. The IM module can also be used to manage maintenance programs. IM uses a hierarchy and includes budget and planning functionality. Its great strength is reporting of a portfolio of projects (or orders) through an enterprise.

☞ QUESTION 62

Account assignment in PR for WBS

I would like to attach a WBS to a PR. I would like to know whether I should use account assignment P or Q. Before I make the decision though, I would like to know as much background on the functions of both.

Is there a significant difference between the two?

✐ ANSWER

The definition for both is simple. P is used for services, while Q is for materials. And the difference lay in their definition.

☞ QUESTION 63

Distribution Cycle

I need to distribute some costs on WBS. I tried to use transaction KSV5 "Execute actual distribution" when I created my cycle on sender section field. However, WBS was not there.

Is there a way to add WBS?

✍ ANSWER

If what you want is to distribute costs from other objects to WBS, then you can very well use the transaction KSV5 after creating the cycle with segments in KSV1.

☞ QUESTION 64

CJ91 - Page Down does not work (BDC or not)

I am using SAP 4.7 and trying to create a BDC to import data related to WBS and Projects from an Open Plan generated flat file.

When I get to the last line in the table control, the code for page down does not work. To my surprise, trying it in the transaction (Not using a BDC) it did not work either.

The only way to page down is to use the scroll bar which does not generate a code in BDC (using the recorder):

RIGHT-ALT and PgDn will place me on the next available line (using the transaction but not the BDC);

The only time the page down does not work is when you have the first page display filled exactly. However, inserting a record would then create one more entry than the page length causing the page down to work again. This is still a bug IMHO.

There does not seem to be a BAPI available to create standard WBS and elements. BAPI_PROJECT_MAINTAIN only deals with WBS, not Standard WBS.

How do I resolve this problem?

✍ ANSWER

You can use LSMW recording and generate the code. Use it in the BDC.

☞ QUESTION 65

Remaining Order Plan

We are currently running 4.7 Enterprise.

I have configured a network type and activated the "planning" indicator.

In OPSV the network type has the "assign funds in plan" indicator turned off.

I still have the remaining order plan included in the assigned value in CJ30 and is therefore consuming my budget.

Is there something I have missed? I do not want the remaining order plan to affect my budget at all for this network type.

The planning indicator on the network type does restrict how the network reacts but it does restrict planning on the network from being included in the assigned value. Further investigation has revealed that the remaining order plan is coming from the plant maintenance orders.

The two reports I am looking at are as follows:

1. Plan/Actual/Comit/remordplan;

2. Budget/Actual/Comit/remordplan;

Both show current year as well as total years. As the budget works by Fiscal Year this remordplan is consuming the current year even if the plan balances out over multiple years.

I am not concerned about these particular reports. All I would like to know is if this ROP values needs to be considered in calculating the Available Budget, functionally. I can always create a custom report w/o this ROP if I am sure that's the value the users are looking for.

For now, we do not have any planning at WBS or Order Level. So is this Remaining Order PLAN still a valid column?

We also plan, and order materials directly from MM.

✎ Answer

Try removing Planning indicator in the OPSC if you have a released PM order that you have planned labor and materials on in 2004. You receive the material in 2004 say 400 dollars. It is now 2005 and you return the material giving you a negative value in the Actuals (-400).

The system calculates Remaining order plan as:

"Plan less Actuals less Commitments";

The plan is zero in 2005, Actuals are negative. The system calculates 0 - (-400) = +400 as the remaining order plan in 2005. It then adds this value to the assigned amount against the 2005 budget on the WBS element it is assigned to.

Also, if the report you are looking at is displaying the Total of Years view, scroll over to the Overall view. You're likely to find that there is no remaining order plan.

If you do not have planned values at all and the ROP is calculated as Plan-(Actual+commitment), then you will observe that it is used only for those with negative values for

Actuals. I was wondering if accounting this ROP as part of Assigned value to calculate the available budget would still be valid though.

Now, with regards your question:

"Do these ROP values need to be considered in calculating the Available Budget, functionally?"

The answer is yes, unless you want to do a system modification. OSS has a note on that. It is better to educate your users on how availability control works. It is there for a reason.

If you are creating purchase requisitions/purchase orders directly from MM you should not have a remaining order plan from materials. If you plan operations or plan stock reservations from within an order, you will have a remaining plan.

Use the transaction opsv to avoid the ROP for the orders with respect to the type.

Lastly, the only solution to clear the existing ROP is to set to TECO.

☞ QUESTION 66

Basic dates on Project Definition and WBS

I have basic dates on my defined project. However, I want these basic dates automatically on the affected WBS element, and also on lower WBS elements.

I thought it was a story of "Top-down" or "Bottom-up" management, but none of them work. Even after scheduling, it still didn't conform to the objectives.

Did I forget or omit something? If so, how do I correct this?

✍ ANSWER

I doubt if the basic dates can be copied from project definition to the WBS elements.

Top down only checks the consistency. But with Bottom up, if you have the "adjust basic dates" indicator set, it would change the basic dates.

You could also put in a substitution rule to copy the dates from the PD to at least your level 1 WBS element. From there, you would manually copy the dates down using the copy function.

Another alternative would be to try using the CJTR_GET_PROJECT_DATES to retrieve the project dates and the function CJTR_POST_DATES for posting dates on the WBS in the user exit (new) created for the substitution module pool program.

SAP Project Systems FAQ

☞ QUESTION 67

Creating a network activity using a BAPI

I am trying to create a network activity using BAPI:

'BAPI_BUS2002_ACT_CREATE_MULTI';

However, I keep getting an error:

'CNIF_PI I078 IProcessing not possible because there is no initialization';

How can I appropriately use this BAPI?

✍ ANSWER

This BAPI has the functionality to create one or more activities of one network only. You have to specify the network for which the activities are to be created in the parameter I_NUMBER (The network can already exist in the database).

To avoid this error you must create a PI (Processing Unit). Each processing unit must be initialized by calling the BAPI "BAPI_PS_INITIALIZATION" once. In your case the BAPI is BAPI_BUS2002_ACT_CREATE_MULTI and the Method is 'NetworkPI.ActCreateMultiple'.

An alternative approach is to try 'bapi_network_maintain'. You can create multiple activities for multiple networks at a given time.

☞ QUESTION 68

Commitment item per WBS

When I set the flag for deletion for the entire item in purchase requisition, the commitment item still appears in the budget. The budget is set per WBS (PS) and all items in PR are of the same WBS.

How can I remove the commitment item from that PR?

Is there any solution to fix this problem so it will not happen again for any PR?

✍ ANSWER

You can run the program RKANBU01 to resolve the problem.

QUESTION 69

Not able to close a project

When I try to close a project (system status CLSD), I get an error saying "There is still a purchase order commitment for this WBS".

How do I correct this problem?

ANSWER

If you have any PO, check the Final invoice indicator which is normally used to reset the commitment.

You may also check if you have a requisition that was created against the project / WBS that has not been converted into a PO.

Lastly, I would suggest running project report S_ALR_87013537 - Commitment Detail report, or CJI5 - Commitment Line items to help identify where the culprit is.

☞ QUESTION 70

How to create a WBS element

When I am doing sales order, the system is asking to enter a WBS element in the account assignment view.

How do I resolve this issue?

✏ ANSWER

First, try to review your settings.

Secondly, check the Account assignment category, which is determined based on the sales document type and the item category group.

SAP Project Systems FAQ

☞ QUESTION 71

A Project with a standard project and network

I want to create a project based on a standard project where I have affected several standard networks and activities. When I tried to do that on CJ20N, only the WBS are created (by copy from standard), and not the networks.

How can I resolve this problem?

✍ ANSWER

When you copy the standard project make sure you select the option with activities button.

Because of the difference data in standard network w/ standard WBS, it will show warning/information message when you create your project. Fix this difference for your network activity to appear.

Add OSS not 695716 to the actual patch SAPKH46C45, and it will be resolved.

☞ **QUESTION 72**

Monthly Budget

We are doing monthly cost planning for WBS Elements using CJR2/Cj40. I have the following questions:

1. Is there any method by which we can define the monthly Budget as well for WBS Elements?

2. Using PS, if I release the budget on a monthly basis, do I need to do it 12 times a year?

I understand we can do it using Cj32 only but how will the availability control work?

It should still be on a yearly basis only.

2. How do I create a funds center?

I do not see anything on Funds Center in 4.7 and if I define the budget here, do I still need to define it in CJ30?

✎ ANSWER

The answers are given according to the order they were asked:

1. A monthly budget can't be done in PS indicated as budget only in overall and annual values. A possible workaround for this is to use the release budget monthly or implement fund management where you can control your payment and commitment budget on monthly basis based on combination of commitment item, fund centre and WBS element.

2. Yes, you must release your budget 12 times a year, availability check will check your released budget accordingly and still on a yearly basis.

3. FM will check the budget based on combination of fund centre, commitment item, fund, and it must be assigned to WBS element.

SAP Project Systems FAQ

☞ QUESTION 73

Settlement Process

I have some questions related to the settlement process:

1. I am collecting costs to level 3 WBS elements and they are all creating different AUC's on release.

   Every month end, we are doing settlement of these WBS Elements to AUC's.

   How will they be settled to one Asset?

   Will all of them have the same settlement rule to settle the costs to the same asset?

   If they are settled to one asset then do i need to enter the asset in each of the WBS Elements manually?

2. I already have default settlement profile (FXA) attached to the Project Definition and the system is generating AUC's for all level 3s. However, it will not be useful if I enter a WBS Element in the Settlement Rule for level 3 WBS Elements.

   Can I settle the WBS Element cost to some other cost object (not AUC) even if it is creating an AUC at release?

   I tried doing it but the WBS is still settling to AUC. I have put Cost Center in the Settlement rule.

3. I have put Cost Center and FXA both in the Allocation

SAP Project Systems FAQ

Structure and the settlement profile also allows settlement to both of these.

The issue is the default settlement is to FXA and when I release a WBS Element, it is creating an AUC. If I enter a Cost Center the Settlement Rule for the WBS Element, the costs are still settling to AUC.

How can this be fixed?

4. Can I make a Settlement Profile field available for input? The field is not available in OPUK/OPUJ.

✍ Answer

Questions are answered in the number they were asked.

1. Yes, but it depends on your version. In 4.70 you can enter the settlement rule at the PD level. It will cascade through your structure.

2. No. There is no valid reason to settle up through the hierarchy that I can see. All you're doing is creating a pile of maintenance and month-end issues, particularly if you are also settling orders.

3. Yes, you can settle to other objects from AUC if your settlement profile is configured correctly.

   If you remove the investment profile, no AUC will be attached so you can choose where to settle to.

   At the end when you want to capitalize the project, you have to create a completed asset; you can do this via the project builder.

Or you can collect costs in the AUC. When you TECO the WBS the costs will clear to the Cost Center. For expense projects you can leave the investment profile out.

4. You can correct separate settlement profiles for each project profile but you cannot make it available for input. You can change it during creation, but that's just making additional work for yourself, not to mention it has the potential for a lot of errors.

SAP Project Systems FAQ

☞ QUESTION 74

Conversion of production order from Unrestricted Stock to Project Stock

We are trying to implement the PS module and we also aim to use project stock. But the problem is we have nearly 5000 production orders that will enter to unrestricted stock after production. For these orders we want to make an account assignment for a project and we want that MRP to see these production orders as entering project stock after production. It is not applicable by writing WBS element in the order by CO02.

What other options should we try?

I have found some fields in AFPO table such as the account assignment of a production order will be changed. I am not sure it will work since some other fields should also be changed.

Is there a way to configure our need for passing from using unrestricted stock to project stock?

✍ ANSWER

Use a material that is set up to trigger the production order and attach this material to a network activity that is set to be reserved for project stock Q and can only be GI to that WBS element. The planned costs are recognized in the project but the Actuals are only recognized when the finished material is GI back to the project. You can use your planned production orders and MRP in exactly the same way but they are just linked back to the project when they are completed.

If you need to transfer planned orders that are already in place then it can be done in MM. There's a goods movement type specific to where you need to reference the WBS element that is set for requirements grouping.

SAP Project Systems FAQ

☞ **QUESTION 75**

Material Actual Figures

I have the following situation:

I use Movement Type 101 for GR, 281 for GI, Using Valuated Project Stock, Valuated Material, and Item Category L (Project Stock) for creating material component. My report reflects the planned figures on WBS, then breaks on activity then reflects further breakdown at the material breakdown level beneath the activity.

When I do the Actuals i.e. first GR the value goes on WBS, is correct. However, when I do GI it goes on the activity and my material actual breakdown figures don't appear, neither does the commitment column. They remain zero instead and the Actuals GI figure reflects on activity.

What could be causing this and how can I resolve the problem?

✍ **ANSWER**

You need to check your procurement parameters on the material itself.

If the parameters are set to reserve/ purchase the material for a network and not WBS then it will always look for the network number as the controlling object. It is within this section that you decide how you handle the stock, GR/GI, and how it's valuated.

For example, if you have set up your project by contradicting that the project definition has group requirements for a project and then you don't have Q on your special stock indicator on the procurement page, then you will have your costs going in different directions.

☞ QUESTION 76

AFVC- JEST, JCDS

What is the relationship between AFVC table and JEST & JCDS?

✍ ANSWER

The object number provides the relationship between these tables:

You can try se16 to define the relationships.

You can also try the link: 'AFVC-OBJNR = JEST-OBJNR'.

To obtain order/operation with AFVC-OBJNR:

On AFVC-OBJNR read AFVC-VORNR (Your operation number) and read AFVC-AUFPL;

On AFKO-AUFPL = AFVC-AUFPL read AFKO-AUFNR (Your order number);

QUESTION 77

CN23 Relevant Table

I am trying to create a report to show the following:

"Network - Activity - Description - Work Hrs in Activity (Est) - Actual Hrs";

The technical data on the above fields only shows a structure.

Is there a table where this information can be found?

✍ ANSWER

Here is a list that may be of use to your requirements:

For projects: PROJ and PRPS;
For networks and activities: CAUFV, AFVC, AFVU, AFVV, AUFK;
For statuses: JEST, TJ02T, JCDS, JSTO, TJ30T;
For Resources: ESUH, MARC, CRHD, CRHD_V1, CRCO, RESB;
For plan and Actuals try RPSCO;

That should give you a pretty good start to collect the entire project hierarchy the object numbers you will need to access RPSCO and from there collect the plan and actual data.

Or you could just use 12KST1D SAP delivered report which shows you your plan versus Actuals broken down hierarchically right down to the orders, activities, etc.

SAP Project Systems FAQ

Another alternative would be to use following function:

'BAPI_NETWORK_GETDETAIL';

It contains all the fields you are trying to extract in the report. Check it out in SE37.

SAP Project Systems FAQ

☞ QUESTION 78

Restrictions on Availability Control

We are currently live with 4.7 Enterprise without implementation of FM or GM.

We are currently using PS budgeting/supplements/returns and have the following availability control features: warning with e-mail at 80 percent and hard error at 100 percent.

Client request is to continue with this strategy with the following changes: Warning with e-mail at 80 percent to continue and that hard error at 100 percent be restricted to material and miscellaneous costs only. The warnings with e-mail are also to be continued through 100 percent for any labor costs.

Labor costs can be identified by G/L account used but if I exempt the G/L from availability control then it is also excluded from consuming the budget at all. The client wants "labor to consume the budget" just react differently than other costs when availability control kicks in.

I then looked into identifying labor costs by transaction using availability control activity groups. However the standard delivered ones do not include CATS transfers. I have looked all over the SAP help and they only refer to creating new entries in the activity groups from within FM or GM. I can find no way to do it from within PS.

As a further note, labor costs can also originate from a journal voucher transfer which is another issue I need to address. Even if I can create an activity group for CATS I, still need to

SAP Project Systems FAQ

identify specifically the labor costs from journal vouchers.

How can I possibly accomplish the client's requirements?

✍ Answer

The answer from the OSS was this:

You should use the customer exit CATS0003: "Validate recorded data' as there is no direct means of activating the necessary check.

Using this exit, you can validate any entered data against the status BUDG.

☞ QUESTION 79

IM/PS transaction IME0

Does anyone know which tables are used in transaction IME0??

I know for transaction CJE0 table RPSCO is used but for transaction IME0 it is a big mystery.

✍ ANSWER

You will not find it using one single table. The main reference is the cluster table COIX (Controlling: Info system cluster tables). This includes RKDTYPCX.

☞ QUESTION 80

Planned revenue

We are facing a problem related to Planned Revenue.

We are creating WBS element, activity and activity milestones. These milestones are getting copied in a billing plan in Sales order and WBS element is given in the account assignment at item level. However, I am still not getting the planned revenues in any of the standard PS report.

What am I doing wrong and how do I resolve this problem?

✍ ANSWER

You can do the following to backtrack a little bit to review some procedures you might have missed.

1. Check the PS Planning profile, so that the flag indicating the adoption of revenue plan from the Sales documents is on.

2. You can also check the Billing element (Operative Indicator) for the WBS which you have mentioned in the Sales order.

3. Check the customizing procedure for revenues:

    "Planned revenues - Automatic calculation... - Update from SD";

    You have to mark this if you want to have an update data from SD.

SAP Project Systems FAQ

☞ QUESTION 81

Down load PS report in XLS

We are getting Export (Gray Shade) in Menu.

Can we download to XLS of all reports such as S_ALR_87*?

✍ ANSWER

Yes, you can download the maximum as html format and open this file in Excel.

You can also try Menu path Report>Export & then entering a filename with the extension .DAT. From there, you can then open the file from Excel.

There should be an option when downloading to a spreadsheet format. There is a program that must be run in each system and when that is complete, you can run excel directly in the SAP screen [which includes an option to save].

☞ QUESTION 82

LOE activity

How is the BCWP calculated in the case of LOE activities?

✍ ANSWER

For the LOE method, the BCWP is calculated in the exact same way that BCWP for that object was calculated: if the object uses cost proportionality for planned EV, then it uses cost proportionality [with planned costs] to calculate BCWP. The end result is that BCWP = BCWS.

☞ QUESTION 83

BCWS and BCWP not calculated

When I run CNE1 and then CNSE5 I check that my POC values are correct, but still, BCWS and BCWP are not calculated and maintain the value 0.

I've created Value category in OPI1 and assigned it to a secondary cost element (category 61) in OPI2. Then I've assigned cost element to a cost element group.

At the end, I run CNE1 and CNSE5 and BCWS and BCWP remain with value 0.

How can I fix this?

✎ ANSWER

There is a check report available that will allow you to make sure the configuration is complete -> CHECKREPORT_PROGRESSANALYSIS, run this from SE38.

One common omission is that the EV cost elements are not assigned to a cost element group. You can link the EV cost elements to the cost elements used on the project plan in the IMG under the progress analysis tab.

If you feel that the configuration is correct, double check that the objects have EV methods and the progress version assigned. Then, as a last resort, check table COSB and see if any values show up. If they do not, then it is related to EV setup. If values do show up, then it is related to the reporting/value category setup.

QUESTION 84

Remove mandatory field, bus area project profile for STD project

We want to remove the mandatory field for the business area in a standard project profile (template). We have linked with CC to BA in configuration.

Are we on the right track?

ANSWER

Your business area is set to mandatory to satisfy FI posting requirements. You either have to use a default BA that the user will have to override or create separate project profiles for each business area.

Furthermore, you can set the BA field to be an optional field or hide it in the profile.

To change the field selection on the templates go to the following transactions:

OPUH - Standard project definition - BA Field - PROJ-VGSBR

OPUI - Standard WBS element - BA Field - PRPS-PGSBR

When posting a transaction, check all requirements including FI field status and if it is set as required anywhere else then it is required everywhere else and so you must comply.

QUESTION 85

Milestone completion Report

We are getting the materials manufactured through subcontracting and in-house production for projects.

Is there a report on the completion of milestone activities for periodic monitoring?

ANSWER

You can use standard report cn53n wherein you can display the actual completion date of your milestone. With a small modification with work flow you can make confirmations of your milestone to trigger change user status your project.

You only need to monitor in project level so it is easier for your user.

An alternative approach would be to use the canned milestone or activity overview reports. Setup the columns to give you the information you need and save as your own variant. You should identify whether the activity has been completed if there is an actual date or a mcnf status.

QUESTION 86

Link between PS and MM

What are the integration points between PS and MM?

ANSWER

There are several points of integration between PS and MM. Some of them are as follows:

- PRs created from PS;
- Reservations created from PS;
- MRP run for PS project stock;

Usually, the link is attached to MM via the reference point. Anything in line with that reference point is now integrated, such as the account assignment number, activity, etc.

☞ QUESTION 87

Economics for PS

Is it possible to calculate in PS the TIR, PNV (net value present) for a project?

✍ ANSWER

Before anything is started, you need to determine what the calculation will be based on. The possibility or non-possibility depends on the basis.

The worst scenario would be to create a custom report that performs the calculations.

☞ QUESTION 88

Customizing detail screen for Definition project

Is it possible to define the layout of Definition project detail screen, as we do on WBS element detail screen?

✍ ANSWER

Yes, it is possible.

The Project Definition layout is in IMG path: PS-> Structures -> Operative Structures-> WBS-> User Interface Settings-> Define Field selection for WBS.

There will appear a panel pop-up to choose activity for Project Definition or WBS element.

☞ QUESTION 89

PS report to see all goods movements linked to one project

Is there such a report to see all goods movements linked to one project?

By goods movements I mean goods issues, etc.

✎ ANSWER

Yes there is. Try running cn52.

SAP Project Systems FAQ

☞ QUESTION 90

PR and Reservations

I have some requirements to fulfill:

1. Charge the project immediately during goods receipt
2. Creation of PR and Reservations from PS
3. Issuance is made against reservations
4. No MRP

Questions:

1. How can I create a PR and reservation from PS?

I need the PR and reservation to be created simultaneously.

2. Do I use "No project Stock" option as opposed to "Valuated Stock" and "Non-Valuated Stock"?

When I use "No Project Stock", it seems that when I choose N-Non-Stock, I can only create PR's. When I choose "L-Stock", I can only create reservations.

3. Do I use "N-Non-Stock" or "L-Stock"?

Can someone tell me what the best practice is in procuring for project materials?

The way I see it, users of PS creates Reservations for project stock and let MRP do the buying. Receipt will be to project stock.

4. Will it show in project Actuals?

✍ ANSWER

In a project, when you choose stock item to supply your material and purchase, the material cost will be charged double to your project.

In other companies, if they order material from stock/warehouse, MRP system will generate PR, PO then gr Po and will add the stock.

The answers to your questions depend on your business processes. There are areas where some materials have to store in stock because the Plant is far from the central city or the purchase process takes a long time.

For valuated and non valuated, non valuated usually is utilized for store material after scrap, and repair doesn't have price.

Again, some companies use non valuated material only for maintenance processes. For projects they use new material, because it will have an effect with the asset.

☞ QUESTION 91

Project with AUC and Revenue

We have some projects wherein the cost of a WBS Element has to be settled to Asset. We are also using the same WBS Element to generate revenue for us. Basically asset is belonging to us but is being paid by customer.

Is there a possibility for us to capture this scenario in PS?

There is no Profit Center defined here. CO-PCA is not implemented.

Where will I settle the revenue?

To elaborate further:

> The customer pays us in advance for some work based on the Sales Order. We do the work and as a result, it might bring up an asset for us. We have to recover the cost of the work done only for the customer and not for the asset we bring up as a resultant.

> The problem is that we can not settle cost to profitability as the billing is still not done. Otherwise CO-PCA is not implemented as well. It works only in advance and we can not take this money in Revenue account. We can not settle it completely to Asset as it is only a part of the cost resulting in asset.

SAP Project Systems FAQ

✍ ANSWER

Did you define where you are going to settle the revenue? Most times you settle it to CO-PA or to PCA.

I think this is more a business question than a system question. The bottom line is what the company wants to do with it.

This is because you are saying that this can not settle to revenue since SD billing is not done.

If it is deferred revenue, just settle to a deferred revenue type account to be cleared when you perform the actual billing.

If not, you need to define how the company wants to handle it.

Depending how your company defines what is required, you will need to change your RA Keys to be able to settle to the correct receiver and the clearing process from billing.

You will need to change your RA Keys to allow you to settle Revenue to the Deferred Revenue account.

The basic setting you need on the WBS element that you need to settle revenue and asset is to make sure it is flagged for the indicator that this is a billing element, and has a result analysis key and an investment profile (both on Control Data TAB) defined.

On the settlement rule if your profile is correct you will have the AUC coming automatically (to be changed to an actual asset at the time of capitalization) when you run the first settlement. The revenue will be posted based on the RA Key you have defined.

SAP Project Systems FAQ

Bottom line: The key are the RA Key and the investment profile

Note: You will have to change your settlement profile and here only "trial and error" will tell you the best setup.

☞ QUESTION 92

TAC CNB1 or ME5J with ALV

I am currently using Release 4.6c.

Is there any chance to display the results of the above transactions with the ALV-Layout?

✍ ANSWER

This cannot be done without ABAP programming changes.

☞ QUESTION 93

Project Coding Mask

Can we define a project coding mask with no separator between the Project ID and Project mask?

Can I define it to be continuous PXXXX and not P-XXXX?

I tried removing separators from SP fields in OPSk but it is not working.

Is there a possibility (I mean project coding without separator) of using some other alternative if Standard SAP does not support it?

✎ ANSWER

You already have the answers as stated in your problem.

I can confirm you must have the separator. That is how it recognizes which mask to use. The identifier (which mask) is before the separator and the mask

It is quite possible to have a coding mask without special characters. If you are trying to use any existing mask with which already projects are created, you can not delete it. In such cases, you need to define another coding mask without any special character in between project ID and coding.

An alternative approach would be if you have no coding mask with specific project ID, then you can generate project definition with out special characters.

For example if you have no coding mask for "U", then you can create a project with coding "U1234".

☞ QUESTION 94

Capitalization AUC invest measure to asset from project sy

I used cj88 to post from WBS to AUC investment measure. Can I use the same transaction to perform again to post AUC to final asset since I am going to use the same transaction again?

When I tried normal AUC in assets it indicated that line item settlement is not possible for this asset.

Are there alternatives I can use?

✍ ANSWER

I think this problem occurs because you want to perform line item settlement but your asset class disallowed this. Check your asset class customizing and check the line item settlement in settlement type.

Another possibility is to check your investment profile in investment management set line item settlement to allow you to settle in this type.

Or you can try the following:

In the project builder create a completed asset and put the status of the WBS element in TECO status.

Then run CJ88 again and settlement will execute from AUC to completed asset.

SAP Project Systems FAQ

☞ QUESTION 95

Procedure to capitalize AUC inv measure to final asset

I created Project, WBS elements and used f-02 to post cost to WBS elements. I used cj88 to post to AUC investment measure. I got stuck up here and I am not able to capitalize AUC to final asset as I don't know how to perform it.

What are the transaction codes needed to complete the requirements?

✍ ANSWER

To settle AUC to Fixed Asset, you must maintain your settlement rule with asset number in WBS element (CJ20N), then set WBS status to TECO. Afterwards, perform periodic settlement (CJ88) or perform full settlement in CJ88.

☞ QUESTION 96

Project Settlement to Assets

I want to settle costs from Project to assets. This cost can either be internal labor/time charges or expense costs.

Can I settle time charges to assets using Secondary cost elements [e.g. 650000] or must I only use primary cost elements?

Can someone explain when I should use primary and secondary elements for settlement?

✍ ANSWER

You can settle secondary cost elements to assets without any issues. You just need to make sure you maintain the settlement profile with these cost elements in the source.

QUESTION 97

Posting actual costs to WBS element and settling to AUC investment measure

How do I post actual costs to WBS and settle that to AUC investment measure after creating a project with WBS element hierarchy?

ANSWER

If you work in capex project then it suggests that you must assign investment profile to your WBS (depends on which level in WBS hierarchy acts as AUC). In the Investment Profile, you can define AUC class. This will help you to automatically create AUC when WBS release. This will automatically settle actual cost from WBS to AUc in periodic settlement.

You can also do it by giving the correct settlement rule and then running the settlement.

☞ QUESTION 98

Configure PReq Doc Type for PS-generated Purchase Requirement

I wanted to know if there is a way to configure the Document Type (e.g.: NB). I want this to be automatically generated when creating a Project.

Is this a possibility or not?

✍ ANSWER

Yes, it's possible to change standard document type (NB) for PR in Project System. Check TCode OPTT.

☞ QUESTION 99

Over all Budget and Yearly Budget

We are planning for over all Budgets but need no control on the yearly budget. We want to show the information as budget expenditure and planned budget.

✐ ANSWER

If you want your budget in overall values instead of annual values then check overall values field in your budget profile (TCode OPS9). This indicator will control whether it is possible to plan/budget total values.

INDEX

Account assignment category 87
Activity ID 24
activity 106
actual cost 29,56
Actuals 96
AFPO 94
AFVC 98,99
AFVU 99
AFVV 99
Asset 91,123
AUC and Revenue 116
AUC invest measure 121
AUFK 99
authorization object 49
automatic Sales order 25
automatic sales Quotation 25
Availability Control 101
BAPI 84
Basic dates 83
BCWP 106,107

SAP Project Systems FAQ

BCWS 106,107
BOM explosion 31
BOM Transfer 32
BOM 32
BPEG 47
BPEJ 47
BPGE 47
BUDG 102
budget value 5
business area 108
Capacity Evaluation 71
Capitalize AUC 122
CATA 62
CATS 11,37,64,101
CAUFV 71,99
CJ20 38
CJ20N 63,88
CJ30 89
CJ38 8,72
CJ91 79
CJ9C 55
CJE0 103
CJEQ 6
CJH1 6
CJI5 86
CKIS 30
Classification 7
closed cost 68
CLSD 86
CM01 71

SAP Project Systems FAQ

CMP2	27
CN33	31
CN41	22,46,52,54
CNE1	107
CNF	63
CNMASS	73
CNS41	46
CNS52	30
CNSE5	107
CO02	94
COIX	103
Commitment Detail report	86
Commitment item	85
Confirmation	63
COSB	107
COSP	29
COSS	29
cProjects	28
CRCO	99
create a WBS element	87
CRHD	99
CUNI	67
customer exits	37
Dates	45
Definition project	112
depreciation simulation	34
determine actual date	33
Distribution Cycle	78
Doc Type	125
Download	105

SAP Project Systems FAQ

Economics for PS 111
ESUH 99
external activities 40
externally processed activities 10
extrapolate dates 33
final assets 48
goods movements 113
IME0 103
incoming email 17
Internal NWA 1
internal orders 48
investment measure 122
JCDS 98,99
JEST 98,99
JSTO 99
KKR0 6
KKRC 6
KSV1 78
KSV5 78
level3 18
Loading 38
LOE 106
Long Texts 26
LSMW 38,73
mandatory field 108
MARC 99
Mass change 73
material component item 70
Material Component 58
MB25 61

- 130 -

ME045	44
Milestone	109
Monthly Budget	89
network activity	84
Network number	65
network	25,88
OPI1	107
OPI2	107
OPTP	57
OPUH - Standard project definition	108
OPUI - Standard WBS element	108
OSS	102
Over all Budget	126
Page Down	79
PCNF	63
Phase Plan	1
plan cost	29
Planned revenue	104
posting date	72
Posting	124
PR	44,114
production order	94
Profit Center	116
profit centers	68
PROJ	99
project accounting	28
Project Coding Mask	120
Project Definition	83
project planning	28
project profile	108

Project Settlement 123
Project stock 12,94
Project System 28
Project version 4
PRPS 16,99
PS and MM 110
PS Authorization 2
PS Confirmations 64
PS conversions 38
PS Document 8
PS Substitution 23
Purchase Requisition 40,61,125
READ_TEXT 26
Rem Order Plan 42
Remaining Order Plan 80
RESB 99
Reservation 61,114
RPSCO 6,29,47,99,103
SD x PS 25
SE37 100
settle 74
Settlement Process 91
Settlement to assets 18
shd0 72
SMOD 37
Stage Gate Methodology 28
stock reservation 61
sub networks 57
Subcontracting 13
Substitution 16

T162K 44
table 99
TECO 49
Time Transfer to Target 62
TJ02T 99
TJ30T 99
transaction variant 72
Transport Request 60
Unit costing 30
Unrestricted Stock 94
USER FIELDS 16
User Status 49
Valuated Material 96
Valuated Project Stock 96
Value based commitment 66
WBS element 7,20,53,91,104,116,124
WBS Plan 47
WBS 26,96
Work Breakdown Structure 28
WorkForce Planning 27
Yearly Budget 126

Attention SAP Experts

Have you ever considered writing a book in your area of SAP? Equity Press is the leading provider of knowledge products in SAP applications consulting, development, and support. If you have a manuscript or an idea of a manuscript, we'd love to help you get it published!

Please send your manuscript or manuscript ideas to jim@sapcookbook.com – we'll help you turn your dream into a reality.

Or mail your inquiries to:

Equity Press Manuscripts
BOX 706
Riverside, California
92502

Tel (951)788-0810
Fax (951)788-0812

50% Off your next SAPCOOKBOOK order

If you plan of placing an order for 10 or more books from www.sapcookbook.com you qualify for volume discounts. Please send an email to books@sapcookbook.com or phone 951-788-0810 to place your order.

You can also fax your orders to 951-788-0812 .

SAP Project Systems FAQ

Interview books are great for cross-training

In the new global economy, the more you know the better. The sharpest consultants are doing everything they can to pick up more than one functional area of SAP. Each of the following Certification Review / Interview Question books provides an excellent starting point for your module learning and investigation. These books get you started like no other book can – by providing you the information that you really need to know, and fast.

SAPCOOKBOOK Interview Questions, Answers, and Explanations

ABAP	-	SAP ABAP Certification Review: SAP ABAP Interview Questions, Answers, and Explanations
SD	-	SAP SD Interview Questions, Answers, and Explanations
Security	-	SAP Security: SAP Security Essentials
HR	-	mySAP HR Interview Questions, Answers, and Explanations: SAP HR Certification Review
BW	-	SAP BW Ultimate Interview Questions, Answers, and Explanations: SAW BW Certification Review
	-	SAP SRM Interview Questions Answers and Explanations
Basis	-	SAP Basis Certification Questions: Basis Interview Questions, Answers, and Explanations
MM	-	SAP MM Certification and Interview Questions: SAP MM Interview Questions, Answers, and Explanations

SAP BW Ultimate Interview Questions, Answers, and Explanations

Key Topics Include:

- The most important BW settings to know
- BW tables and transaction code quick references
- Certification Examination Questions
- Extraction, Modeling and Configuration
- Transformations and Administration
- Performance Tuning, Tips & Tricks, and FAQ
- Everything a BW resource needs to know before an interview

mySAP HR Interview Questions, Answers, and Explanations

Key topics include:

- The most important HR settings to know
- mySAP HR Administration tables and transaction code quick references
- SAP HR Certification Examination Questions
- Org plan, Compensation, Year End, Wages, and Taxes
- User Management, Transport System, Patches, and Upgrades
- Benefits, Holidays, Payroll, and Infotypes
- Everything an HR resource needs to know before an interview

SAP SRM Interview Questions, Answers, and Explanations

Key Topics Include:

- The most important SRM Configuration to know
- Common EBP Implementation Scenarios
- Purchasing Document Approval Processes
- Supplier Self Registration and Self Service (SUS)
- Live Auctions and Bidding Engine, RFX Processes (LAC)
- Details for Business Intelligence and Spend Analysis
- EBP Technical and Troubleshooting Information

SAP MM Interview Questions, Answers, and Explanations

- The most important MM Configuration to know
- Common MM Implementation Scenarios
- MM Certification Exam Questions
- Consumption Based Planning
- Warehouse Management
- Material Master Creation and Planning
- Purchasing Document Inforecords

SAP Project Systems FAQ

SAP SD Interview Questions, Answers, and Explanations

- The most important SD settings to know
- SAP SD administration tables and transaction code quick references
- SAP SD Certification Examination Questions
- Sales Organization and Document Flow Introduction
- Partner Procedures, Backorder Processing, Sales BOM
- Backorder Processing, Third Party Ordering, Rebates and Refunds
- Everything an SD resource needs to know before an interview

SAP Basis Interview Questions, Answers, and Explanations

- The most important Basis settings to know
- Basis Administration tables and transaction code quick references
- Certification Examination Questions
- Oracle database, UNIX, and MS Windows Technical Information
- User Management, Transport System, Patches, and Upgrades
- Backup and Restore, Archiving, Disaster Recover, and Security
- Everything a Basis resource needs to know before an interview

SAP Project Systems FAQ

SAP Security Essentials

- Finding Audit Critical Combinations
- Authentication, Transaction Logging, and Passwords
- Roles, Profiles, and User Management
- ITAR, DCAA, DCMA, and Audit Requirements
- The most important security settings to know
- Security Tuning, Tips & Tricks, and FAQ
- Transaction code list and table name references

SAP Workflow Interview Questions, Answers, and Explanations

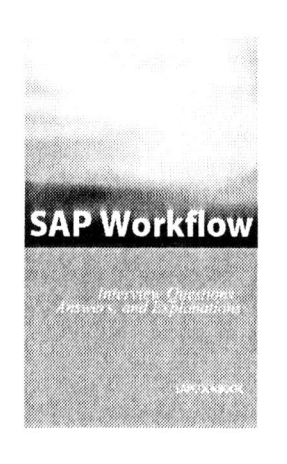

- Database Updates and Changing the Standard
- List Processing, Internal Tables, and ALV Grid Control
- Dialog Programming, ABAP Objects
- Data Transfer, Basis Administration
- ABAP Development reference updated for 2006!
- Everything an ABAP resource needs to know before an interview